Pickleball Strategy and Doubles

The A-Z Guide to Mastering Winning Strategies, Equipping New Players with Rules, Racket Techniques, Etiquette, and Tips for Doubles to Win

© **Copyright 2023 - All rights reserved.**

The content contained within this book may not be reproduced, duplicated, or transmitted without direct written permission from the author or the publisher.

Under no circumstances will any blame or legal responsibility be held against the publisher, or author, for any damages, reparation, or monetary loss due to the information contained within this book, either directly or indirectly.

Legal Notice:

This book is copyright protected. It is only for personal use. You cannot amend, distribute, sell, use, quote, or paraphrase any part of the content within this book without the consent of the author or publisher.

Disclaimer Notice:

Please note the information contained within this document is for educational and entertainment purposes only. All effort has been executed to present accurate, up-to-date, reliable, and complete information. No warranties of any kind are declared or implied. Readers acknowledge that the author is not engaging in the rendering of legal, financial, medical, or professional advice. The content within this book has been derived from various sources. Please consult a licensed professional before attempting any techniques outlined in this book.

By reading this document, the reader agrees that under no circumstances is the author responsible for any losses, direct or indirect, that are incurred as a result of the use of the information contained within this document, including, but not limited to, errors, omissions, or inaccuracies.

Table of Contents

Introduction 1

Chapter 1: The Basics of Pickleball 4

Chapter 2: Equipping for Double Play 15

Chapter 3: The Fundamentals of Double Play 29

Chapter 4: Pickleball Strategies and Tactics 39

Chapter 5: Developing Racket Techniques 52

Chapter 6: The Mental Game and Strategy Execution 66

Chapter 7: Advancing Your Skills in Double Play 78

Chapter 8: Beyond the Basics: Playing Smart and Winning 88

Conclusion 96

References 98

Introduction

Imagine a world where the sun always shines, laughter fills the air, and pickleball is not just a sport but an exhilarating adventure. In this world, your paddle becomes a magic wand, and your moves are pure wizardry on the court. Welcome to the realm of *"Pickleball Strategy and Doubles,"* a book that promises to be your ticket to a thrilling, high-spirited pickleball journey like no other.

This book is more than an ordinary guide. It's your personal pickleball genie. Its mission is to transform you from a novice to a pickleball maestro. Whether you're just starting out or looking to enhance your skills, this book is designed to make your pickleball dreams come true.

You might wonder what makes this book different from the plethora of pickleball guides on the market. Here's why *"Pickleball Strategy and Doubles"* stands out:

- **Easy to Understand:** Say goodbye to confusing jargon and complex theories. This guide speaks your language. It's written in a way that even the newest of newcomers can grasp. You won't need a pickleball dictionary because this book is crystal clear.

- **Perfect for Beginners**: If you're new to pickleball, this book is your perfect starting point. It takes you by the hand and guides you through the basics, ensuring you have a solid foundation to build upon.

- **Hands-On Methods and Instructions:** Forget boring theory without practical applications. This book is all about hands-on learning. It provides actionable, step-by-step instructions that will have you swinging your paddle confidently in no time.

- **Unlock the Secrets**: Inside these pages, you'll find secrets that aren't just for the pros. These hidden gems are for you, the pickleball enthusiast who's ready to shine. Discover the strategies and techniques that will leave your opponents in awe.

- **Fun and Engaging**: Learning should be fun, right? *"Pickleball Strategy and Doubles"* makes sure of that. It's designed to keep you engaged, entertained, and eager to hit the court. No more dry, boring guides. This book is an exciting adventure in itself.

- **Master Doubles Play:** If you've always wondered how to excel in doubles, this book is your doubles partner. It's packed with tips and tricks to make you and your partner an unstoppable force on the pickleball court.

Imagine serving with confidence, smashing with precision, and defending with finesse. This book is your one-stop shop to achieve all of this and more. Whether you're looking for a fun new hobby, a way to stay active, or you're already a pickleball enthusiast, this book will take your game to the next level.

And the best part? You don't have to wait. The adventure begins the moment you're on the first page. No more standing on the sidelines, wishing you could join in the pickleball fun. It's time to jump into the game with both feet and experience the joy of pickleball excellence.

Chapter 1: The Basics of Pickleball

Pickleball is a sport that combines the best elements of tennis, badminton, and ping pong. In this opening chapter, you'll journey through the foundational aspects of pickleball, from its intriguing origins to the essential rules and court etiquette. Get ready to dive deep into the pickleball universe, where fun, fitness, and friendly competition await!

Unearthing the Whimsical Origins of Pickleball

Pickleball, the sport that's sweeping the world and captivating players of all ages, has a history as unique as its name. This quirky, paddle-based game has a fascinating backstory that takes us back to the summer of 1965 when a group of friends sought to create a game to entertain their children. As you delve into the whimsical origins of pickleball, you'll discover the surprising mix of ingredients that went into crafting this beloved sport.

1. *Pickleball has a fascinating backstory. Source: TheVillagesFL, CC BY-SA 4.0 <https://creativecommons.org/licenses/by-sa/4.0>, via Wikimedia Commons: https://commons.wikimedia.org/wiki/File:Pickleball_Players.jpg*

The Birth of a New Pastime

It all began on Bainbridge Island, Washington, when Joel Pritchard, a congressman, and Bill Bell, a successful businessman, returned from a game of golf and found their kids bored. With a badminton court but no shuttlecock, they decided to improvise. They lowered the net, grabbed some paddles, and used a perforated plastic ball. Little did they know that this spur-of-the-moment decision would birth a new pastime that would eventually take the world by storm.

The first pickleball court was the driveway of Pritchard's home, which they had painted with lines borrowed from the old badminton court. It was here that they began playing what they initially called "badminton with a net." The plastic ball, originally used for another popular family game, had holes in it, which resulted in a distinctive "pop" sound when struck. It was a sound that would become synonymous with pickleball.

The Quirky Name Conundrum

Now, it's time to address the elephant on the pickleball court, the name of the game. Why on earth is it called "pickleball"? The origins of the name are as amusing as the game itself.

The most popular story is the name comes from the Pritchard's' dog, Pickles. Supposedly, Pickles would chase the ball and run off with it, leading to the family playfully calling it "Pickles' ball." And just like that, the quirky name stuck. However, some sources suggest that the dog story might be a part of a made-up story. Joel Pritchard's wife, Joan, once mentioned in an interview that they named the game before Pickles the Dog even came into the picture. The dog tale, although charming, might be nothing more than a clever myth.

A Game That Evolved

Pickleball's evolution didn't stop in the Pritchard's' driveway. It continued to develop, gaining popularity among friends and family. Soon, the game made its way to the local community center, where it was formally introduced to the public. This newfound exposure led to more and more players joining in on the fun, resulting in the creation of rules and a set of guidelines for the game.

Pickleball is often described as a blend of tennis, badminton, and ping pong. The combination of underhand serves, lower net, and the use of paddles instead of rackets gives the game its unique character. Over time, dedicated players refined the rules, scoring system, and court dimensions, shaping the sport into what you know today.

The Global Pickleball Craze

From its humble beginnings on Bainbridge Island, pickleball's popularity has soared to unimaginable heights. It's no longer just a backyard game but a full-fledged sport played in community centers, parks, and professional tournaments worldwide.

In 1976, the first known pickleball tournament took place in Tukwila, Washington, with just a handful of participants. Today, pickleball boasts a global community, and tournaments with thousands of participants are common. The sport has even attracted professional athletes and Olympic champions from other sports who are eager to test their skills on the pickleball court.

Embracing the Fun and Whimsy

What makes pickleball truly special is its commitment to fun and camaraderie. The sport encourages players of all ages and skill levels to join in on the action. The unique combination of skill, strategy, and the "pop" of the ball hitting the paddle makes every game an engaging experience.

Pickleball's roots in family playtime continue to define its spirit. The sense of community, friendship, and inclusivity is unparalleled. You'll often find seasoned players sharing courts with newcomers, offering guidance and tips, and cheering for every great shot, regardless of the player's experience.

As you step onto the pickleball court, you become a part of a quirky and endearing legacy. The sport's amusing origins, with a plastic ball, improvised rules, and a fun-loving approach, have set the tone for an activity that's as much about the people as it is about the game. Pickleball captures the essence of play, sportsmanship, and the joy of sharing moments with friends and strangers alike.

Essential Pickleball Rules and Court Etiquette

Before you delve into the exciting world of pickleball rules and etiquette, start with the basics.

The Equipment

Pickleball is a unique sport that combines elements of tennis, badminton, and ping pong. To embark on your pickleball journey, you'll need three essential pieces of equipment.

2. *Pickleball requires a paddle, a ball, and a net. Source: https://unsplash.com/photos/a-tennis-racket-and-three-tennis-balls-on-the-ground-LOTL-GE7s7o?utm_content=creditShareLink&utm_medium=referral&utm_source=unsplash*

1. **Paddle:** This is your magic wand on the pickleball court. It's slightly larger than a ping-pong paddle but smaller than a tennis racket. Paddles come in various materials, including wood, composite, and

graphite, each offering different levels of power and control. Choose one that suits your playing style.

2. **Ball:** The pickleball itself is a fascinating creation. It resembles a wiffle ball, but it's sturdier and designed for the game. The perforations on the ball's surface make it durable and control its speed and bounce. This unique ball is what adds an element of unpredictability to the game.

3. **Net:** Like tennis, pickleball is played with a net. However, the pickleball net is set at a lower height, just 34 inches in the center, which makes for exciting rallies and dynamic gameplay.

The Court

The pickleball court is similar in size to a doubles badminton court, measuring 20 feet by 44 feet. It's divided into two halves, one for each team, and features a non-volley zone that extends seven feet from the net on both sides. This non-volley zone, often affectionately referred to as the "kitchen," plays a significant role in how the game is played.

The Game

Pickleball is primarily played in doubles, although singles is an option. The game commences with an underhand serve, which must clear the non-volley zone on the other side. The double bounce rule comes into play to add an exciting twist to the game. After the serve, both teams must let the ball bounce once on each side before they can start volleying (hitting the ball in the air). This rule introduces strategy and tactics into the game, preventing players from charging the net immediately after the serve, resulting in longer and more engaging rallies.

Pickleball Rules

Now that you're well-versed in the setup of the game, it's time to explore some essential rules that make pickleball a unique and exciting sport.

Serving Rules

The serving rules in pickleball are quite distinct from other racket sports.

- **Underhand Serve:** When serving, you must hit the ball underhand, and it must be below your waist. This underhand serve is one of the fundamental aspects of pickleball, and it creates a level playing field for players of all skill levels.

- **Serving Square**: Unlike tennis, where you serve diagonally across the court, in pickleball, you serve diagonally to the opponent's service square. It's a subtle but important difference that sets the game apart and makes for engaging exchanges.

- **No Bounce in Kitchen**: The ball must not land or bounce in the non-volley zone (kitchen). If it does, it's considered a fault. This rule adds an extra layer of strategy to the game, as the server needs to clear the kitchen while also targeting the opponent's service square.

Double Bounce Rule

One of the most distinctive rules in pickleball is the double bounce rule. After the serve, both teams must let the ball bounce once on each side before they can start volleying. This rule adds strategy and tactics to the game, preventing players from rushing the net immediately after the serve. It ensures that rallies are longer and more engaging, creating an enjoyable playing experience for all skill levels.

Non-Volley Zone (Kitchen) Rules

The non-volley zone, often affectionately referred to as the "kitchen," has its own set of rules:

- You can't volley (hit the ball in the air) from the kitchen. This rule encourages players to engage in shorter, more strategic shots like dinks and drops, making the game all the more exciting.

- You can't step into the kitchen while volleying, even if you manage to keep your feet out of it. This rule ensures that players stay clear of the kitchen while volleying to maintain the integrity of the game.

- You can enter the kitchen after the ball has bounced once on both sides of the court. The kitchen is a strategic area, and players often find themselves locked in a game of skill and finesse as they try to outmaneuver their opponents near the net.

- The kitchen is a crucial part of pickleball strategy, and knowing how to navigate it can make all the difference in your gameplay.

Faults and Scoring

In pickleball, a fault is any violation of the rules. It includes hitting the ball out of bounds, not clearing the kitchen on the serve, or stepping into the kitchen while volleying. A fault results in a side-out, which means the opposing team gets the chance to serve.

Scoring and Winning

Scoring in pickleball is a bit different from some other racket sports. You only score when you're serving, and games are typically played to 11 points. However, if both teams reach 10 points, the game continues until one team leads by at least two points. It leads to nail-biting finishes and ensures that a game swings in either direction until the very end. It's this unique scoring system that makes pickleball so thrilling and competitive.

The Unspoken Language of Pickleball Etiquette

It's time to venture into the world of pickleball etiquette. While the rules are crucial, the unspoken etiquettes are what make the game a friendly and enjoyable experience.

- **Good Sportsmanship**: In any sport, including pickleball, good sportsmanship is the golden rule. Remember that while the game gets competitive, it's ultimately just a game. Respect your opponents and treat every match as an opportunity to have fun. Nobody likes a sore loser or a gloating winner, and the heart of pickleball is in the camaraderie.

- **Acknowledgment:** Begin each game by acknowledging your opponents. A friendly nod or a quick greeting sets the tone for an amicable match. This simple gesture creates a sense of community on the court and fosters a positive playing environment.

- **Kitchen Decorum:** The non-volley zone, or kitchen, is a crucial area on the pickleball court. Following kitchen rules is not only a matter of etiquette but also strategy. In the heat of play, it will be tempting to step into the kitchen to make a play, but remember that doing so is a violation of the rules. The kitchen serves as a strategic battlefield where players use finesse shots and drinks to outmaneuver their opponents near the net. By respecting the kitchen rules, you maintain the integrity of the game and enhance the excitement of play.

- **Score Calling:** When calling the score, do it loudly and clearly. It helps everyone, including your opponents, keep track of the game's progress. Clear score communication is essential, as it avoids confusion and ensures both teams are on the same page regarding the score.

- **Communication:** Communication with your partner is crucial if you're playing doubles. Coordination and teamwork are vital elements of successful pickleball play. Coordinate your movements, call out who will take which shots, and make sure to cover the court effectively. Effective communication turns the tide of a match, and it's an unspoken language that pickleball players understand.

- **Stay Alert:** Pickleball courts are often side by side, and stray balls from adjacent courts make an unexpected appearance. Stay alert and be ready to retrieve stray balls safely, especially if they roll onto your court. It's a matter of courtesy to prevent disruptions to other players and keep the game flowing smoothly. Plus, you wouldn't want to risk getting smacked by an unexpected pickleball!

- **Refereeing:** There may not be an official referee in many casual pickleball games. In such cases, players are expected to self-referee, which means they make calls on their shots and fouls. Honesty and integrity are key. Remember that good sportsmanship extends to fair play, and the spirit of the game relies on players making honest calls, even when it might go against their team's favor.

Pickleball may have a quirky name, but it offers a world of fun and excitement. As you venture into the unique universe of pickleball, remember the rules and etiquette that shape the game. It's not just about winning but building friendships, staying active, and having a good time on the court.

So, the next time you hear, "Pickleball? What's that?" you can proudly say, "It's a fantastic sport, and let me tell you all about it!" With a paddle in hand, a pickleball court as your canvas, and the rules and etiquette in your pocket, you're ready to embark on a thrilling pickleball adventure!

Chapter 2: Equipping for Double Play

As you step onto the pickleball court with your partner, it's a symphony of teamwork, strategy, and shared moments. With your trusty paddles in hand and an unmistakable "pop" echoing off the court, you and your teammate are ready to conquer the non-volley zone, deliver dinks and drives, and craft the perfect plays.

In this chapter, you'll dive into the exciting world of equipping for double play. Equipped with your smiles, high-fives, and the occasional secret signals, you'll dazzle the opponents and create memorable pickleball magic on the doubles court. So, grab your paddles and get started on this fun journey to becoming a doubles pickleball champ.

Pickleball Equipment: The Art of Finding the Perfect Paddle

Pickleball is a game that's easy to pick up and enjoy, making it accessible to players of all ages and skill levels. But before you jump onto the court, there's a crucial decision to make.

Choosing the right pickleball paddle and gear will make or break your game. It's time to explore the world of pickleball equipment and find the perfect gear to elevate your game.

The Heart of Your Game: Pickleball Paddles

At the core of any pickleball player's arsenal is the pickleball paddle. It's your instrument, your extension, and your means of delivering those winning shots. But with a plethora of paddle options on the market, how do you choose the one that's right for you?

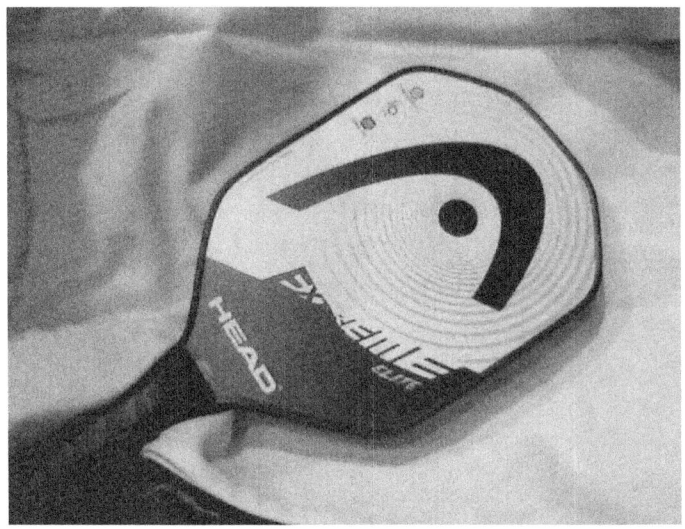

3. *The core of any pickleball player's arsenal is the paddle. Source: Helloheart, CC BY-SA 4.0 <https://creativecommons.org/licenses/by-sa/4.0>, via Wikimedia Commons: https://commons.wikimedia.org/wiki/File:Headpickleballracket.jpg*

- **Materials Matter**: Pickleball paddles come in various materials, each with its unique characteristics. Here are the most common options:

1. **Wooden Paddles:** These are usually the least expensive and great for beginners. They offer good control but may lack the power and spin found in composite or graphite paddles.
2. **Composite Paddles:** Made from composite materials like fiberglass or carbon fiber, these paddles provide a balance of power, control, and touch. They are a popular choice for intermediate players.
3. **Graphite Paddles:** Graphite paddles are known for their lightweight nature and exceptional power. They are favored by advanced players for their quick response and shot versatility.
4. **Nomex Core Paddles:** These paddles are known for their durability and power. They provide a unique sound when striking the ball.

- **Weight Wisdom:** Pickleball paddles come in various weights, and the right choice depends on your playing style. Lighter paddles (around 6-7 ounces) are maneuverable and great for finesse shots and quick reactions, while heavier paddles (8-9 ounces) offer more power and stability. The middle-ground, often called "mid-weight" paddles (7.5-8 ounces), are versatile and suitable for many players.
- **Grip It Right:** The paddle grip size is also essential. A grip that's too small can lead to wrist discomfort, while one that's too large may cause loss of control. To find your ideal grip size, measure

the distance from your palm's lifeline to the tip of your ring finger. Most pickleball paddles come in four grip sizes: 4", 4.25", 4.5", and 4.75".

Get a Grip: Pickleball Grips

The choice of grip for your paddle handle will significantly impact your play. There are two primary types of grips, including cushioned and overgrips.

4. *The grip of your paddle will impact your game. Source: E is for Ian, CC BY-SA 4.0 <https://creativecommons.org/licenses/by-sa/4.0>, via Wikimedia Commons: https://commons.wikimedia.org/wiki/File:Pickleball_balls_and_paddles.jpg*

1. **Cushioned Grips**: These grips are typically more comfortable and absorb sweat well. They are a good choice if you have issues with sweaty palms or want a softer feel.
2. **Overgrips:** Overgrips are thinner and are wrapped over the original grip. They provide a tacky surface, which some players prefer for added control.

The right grip will make your paddle feel like an extension of your hand, so it's essential to find one that suits your preferences.

The Ball's in Your Court: Pickleball Balls

Just as choosing the right tennis ball matters in tennis, your choice of pickleball impacts your game. Pickleball balls come in indoor and outdoor varieties, each with unique characteristics.

5. *Your choice of pickleball paddles can impact your game. Source: E is for Ian, CC BY-SA 4.0 <https://creativecommons.org/licenses/by-sa/4.0>, via Wikimedia Commons: https://commons.wikimedia.org/wiki/File:Pickleball_balls.jpg*

- **Indoor Balls**: These balls are designed for controlled indoor environments and are characterized by smaller holes. They tend to have a softer, less bouncy feel.
- **Outdoor Balls**: Outdoor pickleball balls have larger holes and are built to withstand wind and temperature variations. They are more durable and have a livelier bounce.

Protect Your Assets: Pickleball Gear

Beyond the paddle and ball, other pieces of gear will enhance your pickleball experience:

- **Footwear:** Proper footwear is essential for any court sport. Look for shoes with non-marking soles to protect the playing surface. Consider a court-specific shoe designed for pickleball or other indoor court games for the best support and grip.
- **Sportswear:** Choose comfortable sportswear that allows for a full range of motion. Moisture-wicking materials are ideal to keep you dry and comfortable during intense matches.
- **Accessories:** Accessories like sweatbands, visors, and sunglasses can help improve your comfort on the court. Protecting yourself from the sun and managing sweat will make a big difference in your performance.
- **Try before You Buy:** If you're unsure about the right paddle or gear for you, many pickleball retailers offer demo days where you can try out different paddles to see how they feel. It's a fantastic

opportunity to get hands-on experience and make an informed decision.

- **Don't Forget the Cover:** Once you've invested in your perfect pickleball paddle, it's essential to protect it. Paddle covers are a great way to shield your equipment from scratches and damage during storage or transport. They're an inexpensive but valuable addition to your gear.

- **The Importance of Maintenance**: Pickleball paddles last a long time if properly cared for. Clean your paddles regularly, replace the grip or overgrip when they wear out, and inspect the paddle face for any signs of damage. A well-maintained paddle will perform better and save you money in the long run.

- **Seek Advice from Fellow Players**: Pickleball is a social sport, and your fellow players can be a valuable resource when it comes to equipment recommendations. Don't hesitate to ask for advice and hear about their experiences with different paddles, grips, or gear.

Pickleball is a community. And in this community, the right equipment makes all the difference. Take the time to find the perfect paddle, grip, ball, and gear that suits your playing style and preferences. Remember that while the right gear can enhance your game, the most important thing is to have fun on the court.

Doubles Success in Pickleball: The Winning Playbook

Pickleball doubles is an exhilarating sport that combines the thrill of competition with the joy of teamwork. To excel in this dynamic game, you need a winning playbook that includes the right strategies and a deep understanding of the sport's intricacies. It's time to explore the key concepts and strategies for success in pickleball doubles to help you become a formidable force on the court.

Doubles Basics

In the world of pickleball, doubles play is where the excitement truly unfolds. Here, you and your partner work in tandem to outscore your opponents. Understanding the fundamental aspects of doubles play is essential for success:

- **Communication Is Key:** One of the most critical aspects of playing pickleball doubles is communication. Verbal communication with your partner during a rally is vital to avoid collisions, ensure efficient shot selection, and coordinate strategies effectively. Simple phrases like "mine," "yours," or "switch" make a world of difference in maintaining order on the court.

- **Net Presence**: Controlling the net is a powerful strategy in pickleball doubles. Teams that effectively command this area often have the upper hand. Staying close to the net allows you to cut off angles and apply pressure, making it challenging for your opponents to find openings.

- **Covering the Middle:** The "middle" in pickleball doubles is the area between the two players on the opposing team. Covering the middle is essential to minimize gaps in your defense. It ensures that shots aimed at this region are intercepted or effectively returned, preventing easy winners for your opponents.

- **The Art of Dinking**: Dinking is a subtle yet highly effective technique in pickleball doubles. It involves softly dropping the ball over the net, usually aiming for the opponent's non-volley zone. Dinking helps you gain control of the point, set up your attack, and disrupt your opponent's rhythm.

The Winning Strategies

Now that you've covered the basics, here are some winning strategies that will take your pickleball doubles game to the next level:

- **"Kitchen Control"**: The non-volley zone, often referred to as "the kitchen," is a critical battleground in pickleball doubles. Successful teams aim to dominate this space. Strategically placing shots into the kitchen puts immense pressure on your opponents, forcing errors and securing the advantage.

- **"Poach and Switch"**: "Poaching" involves crossing over to the middle to intercept your opponent's shot. This tactic disrupts your opponents' rhythm and leads to outright winners. Effective poaching requires precise timing and seamless communication with your partner, as you both need to adjust to the changing positions on the court.

- **"The Erne Shot":** The Erne shot is an advanced maneuver that catches your opponent off guard. It involves leaping into the air to hit a ball that's headed out of bounds. While this move requires agility and finesse, it earns you crucial points, leaving your opponents bewildered.
- **"Lobbing":** A well-executed lob can be a game-changer. When your opponents are too close to the net, a high lob will force them to retreat, creating opportunities for you to reposition strategically and gain control of the point. A well-timed lob disrupts your opponents' rhythm and creates openings for your team.
- **"Stacking":** Stacking is a strategic formation where both players on a team position themselves on one side of the court, typically with the stronger player at the net. This configuration creates confusion for your opponents, as they must adapt to unconventional angles and shot placements. Stacking is a tactic that demands coordination and quick transitions.

The Mental Game

Pickleball is not just a physical sport. It's a mental game as well. Your mindset and attitude on the court significantly impact your performance and outcomes. Here are some mental game tips to help you stay at the top of your game:

- **Stay Positive:** Maintaining a positive attitude, even in the face of setbacks, is crucial. A positive mindset boosts your confidence and also lifts the spirits of your partner. It's a game-changer in tight situations and crucial points.

- **Visualize Success:** Visualization is a powerful mental tool. Before a match, take a few moments to visualize yourself executing perfect shots, making strategic plays, and winning crucial points. This mental rehearsal will boost your confidence and improve your actual performance on the court.

- **Learn from Mistakes:** Mistakes are an inevitable part of any sport, and pickleball is no exception. Instead of dwelling on errors or missed opportunities, view them as valuable learning experiences. Analyze what went wrong, discuss it with your partner, and adjust your strategy for the next point or match.

Mastering these mental aspects of pickleball will help you become a more resilient player and a better teammate, which is crucial in doubles play. Your ability to stay composed, encourage your partner, and adapt to changing circumstances makes a significant difference in the outcome of matches.

Practicing for Doubles

Practice is the cornerstone of improvement in pickleball doubles. Here are some practice tips to help you prepare for success:

- **Work on Communication**: Effective communication with your partner is a skill that is honed through practice. Dedicate practice sessions to improving your communication, including calling shots, signaling your intent, and working on positioning strategies.

- **Doubles-Specific Drills**: Engaging in doubles-specific drills simulates actual game situations and helps you develop your net game, quick reactions, and teamwork. These drills include scenarios like practicing the net play, reflex volleys, and transition shots from the baseline to the net.

- **Play with Different Partners**: Playing with various partners exposes you to different playing styles and strategies. This experience makes you a more adaptable player and prepares you for the unpredictable nature of pickleball doubles. It's an excellent way to build your versatility and teamwork skills.

- **The Fun Factor**: While competition is thrilling, remember that pickleball is meant to be fun. The joy of the game comes from playing with friends, making new ones, and enjoying some healthy exercise. Pickleball's social and recreational aspects are as vital as the competitive side. So, whether you win or lose, savor every moment of the game, relish the camaraderie, and celebrate the vibrant pickleball community.

Doubles Etiquette

Pickleball, like any sport, has its code of conduct. Respecting your opponents, partners, and the game itself is essential. Here are some doubles etiquette tips to ensure that the game is played in the right spirit:

- **Good Sportsmanship**: Good sportsmanship is at the heart of pickleball. It entails displaying respect, courtesy, and fairness, whether you win or lose. At the end of a match, always shake hands with your opponents and thank them for the game. This simple act of courtesy goes a long way in building a positive and friendly pickleball community.

- **Line Calls:** Honesty in line calls is paramount. It's a matter of integrity and fairness. Make accurate line calls and give your opponent the benefit of the doubt when a call is uncertain. This level of honesty is expected and cherished in the pickleball community.

- **Stay Hydrated**: Hydration is crucial to maintaining your performance on the court. Always keep a bottle of water nearby, and take short breaks when needed to stay refreshed. Staying properly hydrated ensures you're at your best at every point.

Pickleball doubles is a sport that combines strategy, teamwork, and skill, making it challenging and incredibly enjoyable. Focusing on the basics, implementing winning strategies, practicing diligently, and maintaining a positive attitude prepare you for success on the court.

In this chapter, you've explored the essentials of gearing up for doubles play. Your choice of paddle, gear, and your approach to communication and strategy significantly impact your performance on the court. Now, with your equipment sorted and a game plan in mind, you're all set for the exhilarating world of doubles pickleball.

Get ready to rally, strategize, and celebrate the joy of playing alongside a partner. Doubles pickleball is a dynamic dance of coordination and teamwork. Grab your gear, communicate with your partner, and hit the court for some pickleball magic!

Chapter 3: The Fundamentals of Double Play

In the thrilling world of pickleball doubles, the fundamentals are the key to success. Just like any great team sport, it all starts with positioning. Ensuring you and your partner are in the right place at the right time maximizes control over the court and creates a seamless flow of play. As the game unfolds, communication becomes your secret weapon. Keeping the conversation going with your partner is like having a built-in GPS guiding you both to victory.

Your winning moves are anticipating your opponents' moves, coordinating your shots, and striving for 100% accuracy on serves. Remember, it's not about power but about placement. When you master these basics, you'll be dancing on the court, and that's what makes pickleball doubles a true delight. In this chapter, you'll explore the fundamentals of double play. So, grab your paddle, find your partner, and let the fun-filled pickleball adventure begin.

Understanding the Dynamics of Doubles in Pickleball

Pickleball's fast-paced nature and friendly competition make it a favorite among players of all ages. While singles play is exciting, the true essence of pickleball shines in doubles matches. Understanding the dynamics of doubles in pickleball is all about synergy, communication, and strategic finesse that will elevate your game to new heights.

6. *Pickleball's fast-paced and friendly competition makes it a favorite among players of all ages. Source: https://unsplash.com/photos/a-group-of-people-play-tennis-UHZ_w1bOIvY?utm_content=creditShareLink&utm_medium=referral&utm_source=unsplash*

Court Positioning

Strategic positioning is a game-changer in pickleball doubles. The court is divided into left and right, with each player responsible for their respective side. Staying close to the middle, known as the "centerline strategy," allows players to cover the court efficiently and react swiftly to opponent shots.

- **Centerline Strategy:** Positioning yourselves close to the center reduces the gaps opponents can exploit. This allows you to cover a larger part of the court, reducing the need for extreme lateral movement.

- **Staggered Stance:** In the ready position, stand in a staggered stance, with one player slightly ahead. This position optimizes reaction time and court coverage.

- **Active Movement:** Don't be static. Always be prepared to move with your partner. As the ball moves, your positioning should adjust accordingly. If one player moves forward, the other should move backward to maintain court coverage.

- **Communication and Movement:** Effective positioning is closely tied to communication. Your movement should be synchronized with your partner's. When they move, you move, maintaining proper court coverage.

Net Play and Dinking

Net play is often the highlight of pickleball doubles. Mastering the art of dinking and volleying at the net is crucial for putting pressure on opponents and creating opportunities.

- **Dinking:** The dink, a soft shot just clearing the net, is a powerful tool. It forces your opponents into making errors or setting up opportunities for smashes. The key to a successful dink is to keep it low and just over the net, making it challenging for opponents to attack.

- **Volleying:** The volley, hitting the ball in the air before it bounces, is a weapon at the net. It allows for quick and aggressive plays. Combining volleys with dinks creates a dynamic strategy, keeping opponents on their toes.

- **Smashes:** Occasionally, an overhead smash is a game-changer. Timing is critical. A well-executed smash will surprise opponents and win points.

- **Defensive Net Play**: Net play isn't just about offense. It's also about defending against aggressive opponents. Being prepared to block and return fast shots at the net is vital.

Anticipate and Adapt

Anticipation is a skill that separates great players from good ones. Observing opponents' movements, shot patterns, and body language provide valuable insights.

- **Observing Opponents:** Pay attention to how your opponents play. Do they favor backhand shots? Are they aggressive at the net? Understanding their tendencies can help you anticipate their moves.

- **Shot Patterns:** Recognize the patterns in your opponents' shots. If they consistently aim for the baseline, be ready for it. If they frequently use lobs, position yourselves accordingly.

- **Body Language:** Watch your opponents' body language. It will provide cues about their intentions. A slight shift in weight or racket angle reveals where they're planning to hit the ball.

- **Adaptability:** Flexibility in strategy and shot selection is essential. Be ready to adapt to different opponents' styles during a match. If a particular tactic isn't working, change it up to keep your opponent guessing.

Mental Fortitude

Pickleball is as much a mental game as it is physical. Maintaining composure during intense rallies, bouncing back from setbacks, and staying focused on the game plan is vital.

7. *Maintaining a positive attitude can uplift the team spirit. Source: https://pixabay.com/photos/board-chalk-feedback-review-study-3700116/*

- **Stay Positive**: A positive attitude, even in challenging situations, can uplift the team spirit. It's easy to get frustrated after a missed shot, but maintaining a positive outlook will make a significant difference.

- **Resilience:** Bounce back from setbacks quickly. A missed point or a bad rally is in the past. Stay focused on the next point and the game plan.

- **Focused Strategy:** Keep your strategy in mind. During intense moments, it's easy to deviate from the game plan. Stay focused on your strategy and execute it effectively.

- **Celebrate Successes**: Celebrate not just the final victory but also the small successes during the game. It keeps the team's morale high and enhances the overall experience.

In the dynamic world of pickleball doubles, mastering communication, court positioning, net play, anticipation, teamwork, and mental fortitude is the key to success. As you hone these skills and develop a deep understanding of your partner's game, you unlock the true potential of pickleball doubles.

Strategies for Effective Communication

Clear and effective communication is the bedrock of successful pickleball doubles. It involves speaking to your partner and understanding their non-verbal cues. Here are some strategies to enhance communication on the court.

- **Use Simple Signals:** Develop a set of easy-to-understand hand signals with your partner. For instance, a quick tap on the thigh might indicate a switch in position. Simplicity is key, as complex signals lead to confusion.

- **Call the Ball:** Verbalize your intentions by calling the ball early and clearly. For instance, if you're planning to take a shot, a simple "mine" can avoid collisions and misunderstandings.

- **Stay Positive:** Positive reinforcement is a great motivator. Encourage your partner with affirmations like "great shot" or "nice play." It fosters a supportive and uplifting atmosphere on the court.

- **Practice Together:** Dedicate practice sessions to communication. Play rallies where you and your partner focus solely on coordinating your movements and decisions. It's a dance where you both need to be in sync.

- **Analyze after the Game**: Post-game analysis will provide valuable insights. Discuss what went well and what could be improved in terms of communication. Open, constructive feedback is vital for growth.

Teamwork in Action

Now, it's time to dive into how teamwork plays out in the thrilling world of pickleball doubles. It's not just about having a partner but about moving and strategizing as one entity.

- **Court Coverage**: Efficient court coverage is the hallmark of a well-coordinated team. Divide the court into sections, and make sure each player knows their area of responsibility. It reduces gaps and ensures full coverage.

- **Anticipate Each Other**: The ability to anticipate your partner's moves is a game-changer. For instance, if you see your partner moving forward for a volley, be ready to cover the baseline. Anticipation minimizes hesitation.

- **Coordination on Returns:** Effective teamwork shines through in return situations. Communicate whether you'll take the shot or your partner should. This split-second decision-making will make all the difference.

- **The Art of Switching:** Knowing when and how to switch positions is crucial. Typically, the player at the baseline will move to the net when the opportunity arises. Practice this transition to make it smooth and seamless.

- **Covering Weaknesses**: Every player has strengths and weaknesses. A strong team identifies individual strengths and covers for weaknesses. If your partner has a powerful backhand, let them take shots on that side. If they struggle with lobs, be ready to assist.

Doubles Challenges and Solutions

Playing pickleball doubles is a thrilling experience, but it's not without its fair share of challenges. However, these challenges are opportunities for improvement and can be overcome with the right strategies. Here are some common challenges that players face in doubles and the solutions to help you tackle them effectively.

1. **Miscommunication**: Effective communication is the linchpin of successful doubles play. Misunderstandings lead to missed shots, collisions,

and, ultimately, lost points. To address this challenge, you should:

- **Practice Clear Signals**: Develop a set of clear and universally understood signals and hand signs. Whether it's a "Mine" signal for the ball or a specific gesture for where to position, these signals bridge the communication gap during fast-paced rallies.

- **Consistency Is Key:** Consistency in signaling is crucial. When you and your partner use the same signals consistently, it builds trust and reduces the chance of errors. Remember, your opponent is watching, so use signals that only your partner can decipher.

2. **Overlapping Movements**: It's not uncommon for players in doubles to overlap or get in each other's way, leading to confusion and lost opportunities. The key here is staying in sync:

- **Vigilance Pays Off**: Be vigilant about your partner's position on the court. Keep an eye on where they are and adjust your movements accordingly. If they're at the baseline, you might need to cover the net. This mutual awareness prevents overlap and ensures that you cover the entire court effectively.

- **Define Roles:** Clear roles are pivotal in doubles. For example, establish who takes the lead when returning serves or handling lobs. When everyone knows their role, it eliminates confusion and overlapping movements.

3. **Inconsistent Positioning:** Positioning in pickleball is crucial for both offense and defense. Inconsistent positioning leads to gaps in your court coverage. To combat this challenge, be sure to have:

    - **Seamless Transitions:** Moving between positions on the court needs to be seamless. Practice transitioning between the net and baseline, honing your footwork and court coverage. This agility allows you to adapt quickly to the ever-changing dynamics of the game.

    - **Strategic Readiness:** Be prepared for various scenarios. For example, when your opponent launches a lob or a powerful smash, knowing how to position yourself will make a world of difference. Anticipate these situations and practice positioning for each of them.

Addressing these challenges and implementing the suggested solutions will allow you and your partner to navigate the complexities of pickleball doubles more effectively. With improved communication, synchronized movements, and strategic positioning, you'll be better equipped to face any opponent and enjoy a more cohesive and successful partnership on the court. So, keep practicing, refining your communication, and fine-tuning your positioning to overcome these challenges and elevate your doubles game to the next level.

Chapter 4: Pickleball Strategies and Tactics

Strategies and tactics are the secret recipe for success in the exciting sport of pickleball. It's all about outsmarting your opponents. Imagine a blend of precision and power, like a well-mixed cocktail. You've got lobs, dinks, volleys, and the coveted third-shot drop. These are all part of a strategic menu designed to keep your rivals on their toes. And don't forget court positioning. It's the art of being in the right place at the right time.

In this chapter, you'll discover the art of double play in pickleball, where teamwork and strategy become your best allies on the court. Two partners, two paddles, and one common goal to outwit your opponents and seize victory. Double play is where the game's dynamics truly shine, blending the finesse of chess with the agility of tennis. It's about communicating seamlessly with your partner, understanding when to attack and when to defend, and transitioning between these two states with grace and precision.

Winning Strategies for Doubles Play in Pickleball

When it comes to playing doubles, mastering the right strategies makes all the difference between victory and defeat. It's time to explore some of the most effective strategies for doubles play, including the Kitchen Line Dance, the Third Shot, Targeted Shots, and more.

The Kitchen Line Dance

The Kitchen Line Dance, also known as the "dance of patience," is a strategic move to control the non-volley zone (kitchen) and set up your team for success. It involves coordinated footwork and positioning, ensuring you and your partner maintain dominance at the net.

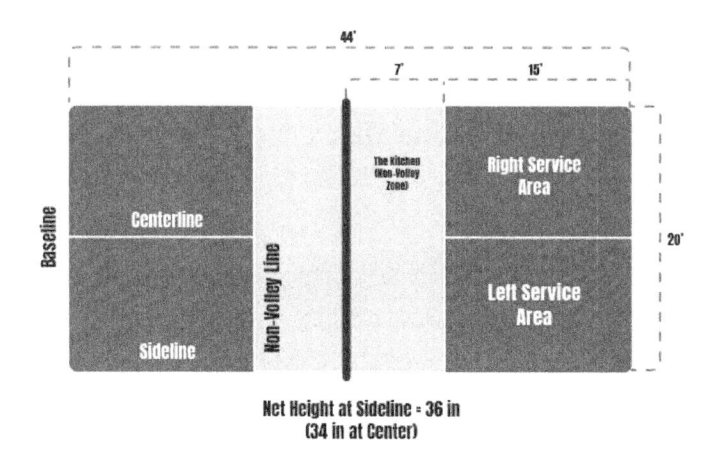

8. *To do the kitchen line dance, you have to start at the baseline. Source: https://cdn.sanity.io/images/jvolei4i/production/4d270fe3506c03 3cff05b06f7c99c95a477e800a-736x450.png*

Step-by-Step Instructions:

1. **Start at the Baseline**: Begin the point by standing at the baseline, one behind the other, with one player slightly off-center to cover the middle.

2. **Advance to the Non-Volley Zone:** Move forward after the serve, taking small steps to stay in sync with your partner. Ensure you both reach the non-volley zone together.

3. **Stay Aligned:** Keep your bodies parallel to the net and maintain an equal distance from the centerline. This alignment maximizes your reach and court coverage.

4. **Control the Kitchen**: Once at the non-volley zone, be ready to volley or dink, but avoid hitting the ball while it's still in the air (a volley). Instead, aim for a dink (a gentle, controlled shot) to maintain control.

Benefits:

- The Kitchen Line Dance allows you to control the net, making it challenging for your opponents to find openings.

- It reduces the risk of making unforced errors by encouraging safe, precise shots.

- Proper footwork and coordination with your partner increase your chances of winning the point.

The Kitchen Line Dance is a fundamental strategy in pickleball doubles. By mastering this dance of patience, you and your partner will create a solid foundation for success on the court.

The Third Shot

The Third Shot is a critical strategy in pickleball that involves the shot you make after the serve and return. It's a transition shot that helps your team move from the baseline to the non-volley zone, setting the stage for control and aggressive play.

A TYPICAL OPENING PICKLEBALL SEQUENCE.

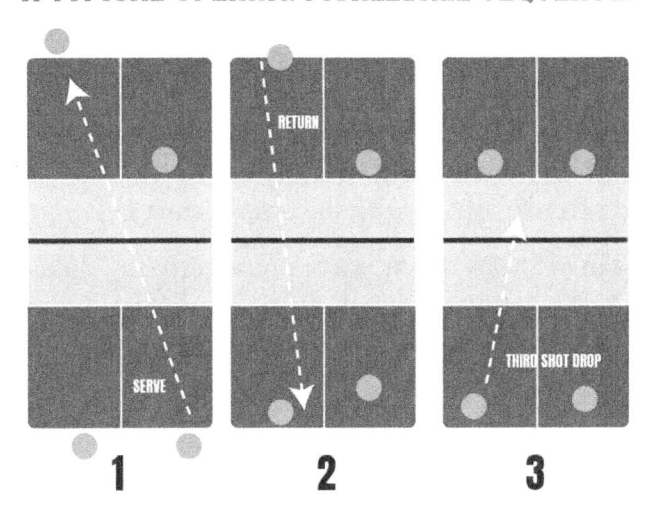

9. *The third shot. Source: https://pickleballkitchen.com/wp-content/uploads/2018/03/visual_threeOpeningShots.jpg*

Step-by-Step Instructions:

1. **Anticipate the Return**: As the server, anticipate where the return is likely to land and be ready to move quickly.

2. **Position Yourself at the Non-Volley Zone:** Start moving forward immediately after your serve, positioning yourself at the non-volley zone.

3. **Execute a Controlled Drop Shot:** Instead of a power shot, aim for a gentle drop shot that lands softly in your opponent's non-volley zone.

4. **Coordinate with Your Partner:** Your partner should also move forward to the non-volley zone, ensuring you both maintain court coverage.

Benefits:

- The Third Shot minimizes the risk of your opponent's taking control of the net and keeps you in a favorable position.
- A well-executed drop shot makes it difficult for your opponents to attack or maintain an offensive position.
- It's a strategic way to transition from defense to offense and establish control over the point.

The Third Shot is a game-changer in doubles play. Mastering this strategy will give your team a significant advantage and set the tone for a successful rally.

Targeted Shots

Targeted Shots involve aiming for specific areas of the court to exploit your opponents' weaknesses or create advantageous positions. Targeting the right spots will help you keep your rivals on the defensive and dictate the game's flow.

Step-by-Step Instructions:

1. **Identify Weaknesses:** Observe your opponents and identify their weaknesses. It could be their backhand, forehand, or mobility.
2. **Aim for the Non-Volley Zone:** Target the non-volley zone (kitchen) to force your opponents to hit difficult low shots.

3. **Play Lobs:** If your opponents are positioned near the net, consider using lobs to force them back and create space.

4. **Mix It Up:** Don't become predictable. Vary your shots to keep your opponent guessing and off-balance.

Benefits:

- Targeted Shots exploit your opponents' vulnerabilities, making it challenging for them to return effectively.

- Playing shots to the non-volley zone can restrict your opponents' options and limit their aggressive play.

- Mixing up your shots keeps your rivals uncertain and under pressure.

Targeted Shots are a versatile strategy that can be tailored to exploit your opponents' specific weaknesses. Using this tactic effectively will give your team a competitive edge in doubles play.

The Poach

The Poach is a doubles strategy where one player at the net moves quickly to intercept a ball intended for their partner. It's a surprise tactic that disrupts your opponents and creates confusion.

10. The poach strategy. Source:
https://www.galeleach.com/pickleball-tips/poaching-done-right

Step-by-Step Instructions:

1. **Anticipate the Opportunity:** Keep an eye on your opponent's shots, looking for opportunities to poach.

2. **Quick Movement**: When you see a shot headed toward your partner, move quickly and decisively to intercept the ball.

3. **Effective Communication:** Communicate with your partner about your intention to poach, ensuring they cover the vacated space.

4. **Aggressive Play**: Once you intercept the ball, be ready to put pressure on your opponents with an aggressive shot.

Benefits:

- The Poach will catch your opponent off guard, leading to unforced errors or weak returns.

- It demonstrates effective communication and teamwork with your partner.
- It will shift the momentum in your favor by creating a more aggressive and dominant position on the court.

The Poach is a strategic weapon that disrupts your opponents and creates opportunities for your team to take control of the point.

Cross-Court Dink

The Cross-Court Dink is a versatile shot that can be employed in various situations to challenge your opponents' positioning and control the pace of the game.

Step-by-Step Instructions:

1. **Position Yourself:** Stand at the non-volley zone, ready to execute the dink.
2. **Angle Your Shot:** Instead of hitting directly at your opponent, aim diagonally across the court (cross-court).
3. **Maintain Control**: Use a gentle, controlled motion to execute the dink, ensuring the ball clears the net and lands softly in your opponent's non-volley zone.
4. **Change the Angle:** Periodically switch between cross-court and straight-ahead dinks to keep your opponent guessing.

Benefits:

- The Cross-Court Dink challenges your opponents' court coverage, making it harder for them to anticipate your shots.
- It allows you to control the pace and rhythm of the game, keeping your opponents on their toes.
- This versatile shot can be used to create openings and exploit weaknesses in your opponents' positioning.

The Cross-Court Dink is a valuable addition to your pickleball arsenal. Incorporating this shot into your gameplay helps you maintain control and keep your opponent guessing.

Quick Switch

Quick Switch is a strategy that involves rapid movement between the non-volley zone and the baseline, effectively changing your team's positioning and putting pressure on your opponents.

Step-by-Step Instructions:

1. **Recognize the Opportunity**: Look for moments when your opponents are vulnerable, such as when they hit a high ball.
2. **Quick Movement:** If the opportunity arises, the player at the net moves back to the baseline, and the player at the baseline advances to the non-volley zone.
3. **Maintain Pressure:** The quick switch disrupts your opponents' expectations and forces them to adjust rapidly.

4. **Stay Aligned:** Coordinate with your partner to maintain proper alignment and court coverage.

Benefits:

- Quick Switch keeps your opponent guessing and prevents them from settling into a comfortable rhythm.
- It allows you to capitalize on vulnerable moments and apply pressure when your opponents are out of position.
- Effective teamwork is essential for a successful Quick Switch strategy.

Quick Switch is a dynamic strategy that unsettles your opponents and creates opportunities for your team to seize control of the game.

In pickleball, winning in doubles play is all about implementing smart strategies. Mastering the strategies mentioned above will increase your chances of success on the court, have more fun, and forge a strong partnership that can withstand any challenge.

Offense, Defense, and Transition Play

The pickleball doubles strategy often revolves around offense and defense. Here is a breakdown of these key aspects:

Offense

Offensive play in pickleball doubles is like orchestrating a symphony on the court. It's about taking the initiative, dictating the tempo, and keeping your opponents on their toes. Here's a more detailed look at offensive strategies:

- **Net Dominance:** Maintaining control of the kitchen or non-volley zone is the bedrock of offensive play. When you control this space, you limit your opponent's options and make it challenging for them to get close to the net.
- **Poach Shots:** Poaching is a clever maneuver where you anticipate your opponent's shot and intercept it with a well-timed volley. It disrupts their rhythm and leads to easy points.
- **Aggressive Net Play:** Sometimes, the best defense is a good offense. Closing in on the net forces your opponents to make difficult passing shots. You apply pressure and are ready to pounce on any weak returns.
- **Attacking the Middle**: Targeting the center of the court is a strategic choice. It creates confusion between your opponents, making it unclear who should respond to the shot, thus increasing your chances of winning the point.

Defense

While offense grabs the limelight, defensive play in pickleball doubles is equally critical. It's all about reacting to your opponent's shots, minimizing errors, and resetting the point. Here are some essential defensive strategies:

- **Lob Returns:** When you find yourself on the defensive, using lob shots will reset the point. Lobs buy you time to regain court positioning and prepare for your next move.
- **Retreating to the Baseline:** Sometimes, the best course of action under pressure is to retreat to the

baseline. From there, you regroup and regain control of the rally.

- **Blocking Shots**: To neutralize the pace of hard-hit shots, blocking is a defensive move that stymies your opponents' aggressive play.

- **High Lobs:** Using high lobs will push your opponent's back, disrupt their rhythm, and create opportunities for you to regain control.

Transition Play

The magic happens when you seamlessly shift between offense and defense, a skill known as transition play. It's where the fast-paced, thrilling nature of pickleball doubles truly shines:

- **Stay in Sync:** To cover the court effectively, both partners must move in unison. Being out of sync leads to openings for your opponents to exploit.

- **Quick Reflexes:** Transition plays often involve rapid exchanges. Your reflexes need to be sharp to respond to fast-paced rallies.

- **Anticipation:** Predicting your opponent's shots is the key to positioning yourself advantageously. It allows you to read the game and react before your opponent's shot even leaves their paddle.

- **Consistent Communication**: Keep the lines of communication open with your partner. A well-timed call or signal will make the difference between a successful transition and a missed opportunity.

Mastering offense, defense, and transition play in pickleball doubles is a dynamic journey that blends strategy with teamwork. With these strategies and tactics, you'll be well-equipped to elevate your game and thrive in the exhilarating world of pickleball doubles.

In pickleball, patience is indeed a virtue, and finding the perfect moment to strike is like a seasoned chef waiting for the ideal moment to add that special ingredient. So, whether you're aiming for your opponent's feet, using depth to your advantage, or perfecting the kitchen line dance, the tactics mentioned in this chapter are the secret ingredients to cook up your victory on the pickleball court.

Chapter 5: Developing Racket Techniques

Mastering your racket techniques in pickleball unlocks the secrets of the game. In this chapter, you'll explore the art of developing racket techniques, a crucial aspect that will significantly elevate your game. Whether you're a beginner looking to establish a solid foundation or an intermediate player aiming to refine your skills, mastering racket techniques is essential to unlocking doubles' success. You'll explore various elements, from fundamental shots to achieving the perfect balance between placement and power.

Mastering Racket Techniques for Doubles Success

Are you ready to elevate your pickleball doubles game and achieve success on the court? Mastering racket techniques is crucial in improving your performance and outplaying your opponents. It's time for you to dive into the key aspects of racket techniques, and find valuable insights and tips for doubles success.

11. Mastering racket techniques can help you elevate your pickleball game. Source: https://unsplash.com/photos/a-group-of-people-play-tennis-UHZ_w1bOIvY?utm_content=creditShareLink&utm_medium=referral&utm_source=unsplash

Grip and Grip Changes

The foundation of effective racket techniques lies in understanding and mastering the grip. The grip is your connection to the racket, influencing control, power, and precision.

Step-by-Step Instructions:

1. **Eastern Grip for Control:** Adopt an Eastern grip for better control over your shots. With the base knuckle of your index finger on the third bevel, this grip enhances maneuverability during fast-paced rallies.

2. **Western Grip for Power:** Transition to a Western grip when looking to add power to your

shots. This grip, with the base knuckle on the fifth bevel, allows for more topspin and potent smashes.

Benefits:

- **Versatility:** Switching between grips provides versatility in your game, allowing you to adapt to different situations.
- **Control and Power:** Mastering both grips ensures you have optimal control for delicate shots and the power needed for impactful drives.

The ability to seamlessly transition between grips is a skill that distinguishes advanced players. Practice both grips regularly to enhance your overall racket control.

Serving Technique

The serve sets the tone for each point, making it a pivotal aspect of doubles play. Mastering your serving technique gives your team a competitive edge.

Step-by-Step Instructions:

1. **Stance and Positioning:** Start with a side-facing stance and position yourself close to the baseline. It provides a better angle for serving specific areas of the court.
2. **Consistent Toss**: Maintain a consistent toss to ensure precision in your serves. Practice tossing the ball slightly in front and to the side for optimal reach.

Benefits:
- **Strategic Advantage**: A well-executed serve can disrupt your opponents' rhythm and set the stage for a favorable rally.
- **Placement Control**: Refining your serving technique gives you better control over ball placement, making it challenging for your opponents to anticipate.

Devote time to perfecting your serving technique because it forms the foundation for initiating successful rallies and gaining a strategic advantage.

Groundstrokes

Groundstrokes form the foundation of a strong pickleball game, allowing players to engage in controlled rallies and maintain court dominance.

Step-by-Step Instructions:

1. **Neutral Stance:** Adopt a neutral stance with your feet shoulder-width apart to maintain balance and mobility.
2. **Forehand Groundstroke**: Execute a forehand groundstroke by turning your shoulders, extending your arm, and making contact with the ball in front of your body.
3. **Backhand Groundstroke:** Master the backhand by using a two-handed grip for added stability. Rotate your hips and shoulders, striking the ball confidently.

Benefits:

- **Consistency:** Groundstrokes contribute to consistent and controlled play, setting the stage for strategic shots.
- **Court Coverage:** Well-practiced groundstrokes enhance your ability to cover the court effectively, responding to shots with agility.

Groundstrokes are the backbone of your game. Practice forehand and backhand techniques regularly to build a reliable foundation for doubles success.

Forehand Technique

The forehand is a versatile and powerful shot, often a game-changer in pickleball doubles. Understanding the proper techniques is essential for success.

Step-by-Step Instructions:

1. **Grip and Stance:** Maintain an Eastern or Semi-Western grip for the forehand. Stand with your feet shoulder-width apart in a slightly open stance.
2. **Swing Path:** Execute a smooth and controlled swing, keeping the paddle face slightly open for topspin. Make contact with the ball in front of your body.

Benefits:

- **Powerful Drives:** A well-executed forehand allows for powerful drives, putting pressure on opponents and creating opportunities for winners.

- **Versatility:** Mastering the forehand provides versatility in shot selection, making you a dynamic player on the court.

The forehand is a potent weapon in your arsenal. Practice consistently to refine your technique and unleash the full potential of your forehand shots.

Backhand Technique

While the backhand may seem challenging, mastering its techniques is crucial for a well-rounded pickleball game. Proper form and execution are key.

Step-by-Step Instructions:

1. **Grip and Stance**: Use a two-handed grip for backhand stability. Stand with your feet shoulder-width apart, turning your non-dominant shoulder toward the net.

2. **Rotation and Follow-Through:** Engage your core and rotate your hips and shoulders for a fluid backhand motion. Follow through the shot with the paddle, finishing at shoulder height.

Benefits:

- **Controlled Returns:** A well-practiced backhand allows for controlled and accurate returns, minimizing errors during rallies.
- **Defensive Strength:** Mastering the backhand provides a strong defensive foundation, enabling you to handle challenging shots with confidence.

Invest time in perfecting your backhand techniques to bolster your defensive capabilities and contribute to a well-rounded doubles game.

Volleys and Smashes

Volleys and smashes are offensive maneuvers that put your team in control of the net and dictate the game's pace.

Step-by-Step Instructions:

1. **Net Positioning**: Move to the non-volley zone (NVZ) to execute effective volleys. Being close to the net allows for quick reactions and minimizes your opponents' response time.

2. **Smash Technique**: Practice the smash by adopting a continental grip and using a short backswing. Aim for a downward trajectory to capitalize on the speed and power of the smash.

Benefits:

- **Net Dominance**: Mastering volleys and smashes grants you control of the net, a position of strength in doubles play.

- **Point-Winning Shots**: Well-executed smashes are potent point-winners, putting pressure on your opponents and forcing defensive plays.

Sharpen your skills in volleys and smashes to become a formidable force at the net, consistently gaining points and controlling the tempo of the match.

Maneuvering the Non-Volley Zone (NVZ)

The NVZ, often referred to as the kitchen, is a critical area where finesse and precision play a vital role in doubles success.

Step-by-Step Instructions:

1. **Quick NVZ Approaches:** Develop agility and quick footwork to approach the NVZ swiftly. It allows you to take control of the kitchen and strategically position yourself for volleys.

2. **Soft Dinks:** Master the art of soft dinks to navigate the NVZ effectively. These controlled shots, barely clearing the net, will force errors from your opponents and set up advantageous plays.

Benefits:

- **NVZ Control:** Efficient maneuvering in the NVZ grants you control over the kitchen, enabling strategic plays and defensive moves.

- **Reduced Errors:** Precise footwork and soft dinks minimize unforced errors, providing your team with a more stable and consistent game.

The NVZ is a dynamic area that demands finesse and quick decision-making. Focus on mastering NVZ techniques to become a reliable and strategic player in doubles.

Mastering racket techniques is a journey of continuous improvement and refinement. Dedicating time to grips, serving, volleys, smashes, and NVZ maneuvers will elevate your doubles game to new heights. Incorporate these tips into your practice routine, stay adaptable on the court, and enjoy the thrill of success in pickleball doubles.

Mastering the Art of Pickleball: Shots, Placement, and Power

Pickleball is a symphony of shots, placement tactics, and well-timed bursts of power. In this journey through the heart of pickleball, it's time to explore the intricacies of each element that transforms a casual game into a thrilling, strategic dance.

Shots That Sizzle

Pickleball offers an array of shots that can elevate your gameplay from a casual hit to a strategic masterpiece.

- **Dinks and Volleys**: The dink, often the unsung hero of pickleball, involves softly tapping the ball just over the net. Mastering this shot allows you to delicately place the ball where your opponent least expects it. Volleys, a seamless transition from dinking, involve swift and controlled hits that will catch your opponent off guard. The dance between dinks and volleys is a game-changer, adding layers to your strategic repertoire.

- **Smashes and Overheads:** The smash, a powerful overhead shot, is the crescendo in your pickleball symphony. It's a shot that demands timing, precision, and a dash of showmanship. Picture yourself standing at the non-volley zone line, eyes fixed on the descending ball, and then, with a burst of controlled power, you send it soaring over the net. It's a declaration of dominance on the court. Overheads are the exclamation marks in your pickleball narrative, turning rallies into moments of pure exhilaration.

- **Lobbing Brilliance:** The lob, a finesse shot that adds an element of surprise, is your artistic expression on the pickleball canvas. Imagine a well-executed lob gracefully arcing over your opponent's head, landing just inside the baseline. It's a shot that combines finesse and strategy, forcing your opponents into desperation as they scramble to retrieve the ball. The lob is a strategic masterpiece that disrupts your opponent's rhythm and sets the stage for your next move.

Placement Magic

While power and precision are essential, knowing where to place your shots is the secret sauce that turns rallies into victories.

- **Target the Kitchen**: The kitchen, that pivotal non-volley zone near the net, is both a challenge and an opportunity. Smart shot placement in this area is a game-changer. Aim for the corners, teasing your opponents into the kitchen, and then deliver a shot that catches them off guard. It's the strategic manipulation of space that defines a skilled pickleball player.
- **Down the Line or Cross-Court**: Variety is the spice of pickleball, and nowhere is this more evident than in shot placement. Whether you opt for the precision of down-the-line shots or the deceptive nature of cross-court placements, varying your angles keeps opponents guessing. Change the game by choosing the right placement at the right

time, and you'll have your opponents on their toes, uncertain of your next move.

- **The Art of Dinking Placement**: Dinking involves placing soft shots with surgical precision. Aim for the edges of your opponent's side, exploit openings, and create opportunities for winning volleys. Dinking becomes a mind game where placement reigns supreme. It's not just about hitting the ball over the net but putting it exactly where you want it, setting the stage for your next move.

Power Play in Pickleball

Power in pickleball isn't a display of brute force. It involves strategically unleashing controlled bursts that catch opponents off guard.

12. *A power play can help you catch your opponents off-guard. Source: Bryceppa, CC BY-SA 4.0 <https://creativecommons.org/licenses/by-sa/4.0>, via Wikimedia Commons: https://commons.wikimedia.org/wiki/File:Newport_Shootout-23.jpg*

- **Powerful Pickleball Serve:** Your serve is the opening act, the first note in your pickleball symphony. Whether you opt for a traditional serve or unleash a spin, use it strategically. Mix up your serves to keep opponents guessing and gain the upper hand. The serve is an opportunity to set the tone and control the rhythm of the match.

- **Hip-Level Power Shots**: Strategically targeting your opponent's hips might sound unconventional, but it's a move that disrupts their rhythm and limits their options. Aiming for the hips allows you to throw a curveball into their game plan, forcing them to adjust quickly. Experiment with this approach and watch as your opponent struggles to return shots effectively. It's a strategic move that combines power with precision.

- **Wrist Snap for Overhead Shots**: Generating power on overhead shots is a finesse game. Practice the wrist snap with both tight and loose grips to find the sweet spot. The wrist snap adds that extra oomph, turning your overhead shots into powerful winners. It requires a controlled burst of power that takes your shots from ordinary to extraordinary.

Pickleball, with its shots, strategic placements, and bursts of power, is a dance where every move counts. Smooth groundstrokes are your go-to move, ensuring the ball glides effortlessly over the net. The forehand becomes your trusty sidekick, delivering winners with panache. Gripping the backhand just right is your secret weapon, unleashing controlled power and consistency. As you engage in volleys, your racket becomes a versatile tool for both defense and offense, a dance of controlled aggression at the non-volley zone. Dinking with finesse turns into an art form, teasing opponents with delicate shots that dance over the net.

As you twirl across the court, experimenting with different shots, surprising opponents with strategic placements, and strategically unleashing bursts of power, remember that pickleball is an art form. Embrace the challenge of perfecting your pickleball racket techniques, and soon, you'll find yourself not just playing the game but painting a masterpiece on the court. So, grab your paddle, step onto the court, and let the magic of shots, placement, and power elevate your pickleball prowess.

Chapter 6: The Mental Game and Strategy Execution

In the fast-paced world of pickleball, where split-second decisions make or break a match, cultivating mental resilience and strategic prowess is crucial. The mental game involves maintaining composure during intense moments, fostering a positive mindset, and developing mental agility. In this chapter, you'll uncover the layers of the mental game of pickleball doubles. From building mental resilience to executing strategies with precision, this chapter is a journey that enhances overall performance.

Building Mental Resilience in Doubles Play

Pickleball doubles is a mental chess match demanding resilience, adaptability, and a winning mindset. As you step onto the court with your partner, aim to smash the perfect shot and navigate the highs and lows with mental strength. It's time to delve deeper into the prime aspects of building mental resilience in doubles play and how a robust mindset elevates your game.

13. Developing mental resilience can help you elevate your game. Source: https://pixabay.com/illustrations/resilience-victory-force-1697546/

The Unpredictable Game

The unpredictability of pickleball doubles is a roller coaster ride. It's a fundamental aspect that separates resilient players from the rest. Here's an exploration of how a mindset shift towards unpredictability turns the uncertainties of the game into opportunities for growth and success.

- **Embracing the Unpredictability:** Seeing unpredictability as an opportunity requires a fundamental mindset shift. Instead of fearing the unknown, resilient players embrace it, recognizing that adaptability is a key factor in success on the court.
- **Thriving in Uncertainty**: Resilient players thrive in the face of unpredictability. They understand that pickleball doubles, with its

constant changes and unexpected moves, is where they can showcase their adaptability and turn the game in their favor.

In the fluid world of pickleball doubles, the ability to thrive in uncertainty can be a game-changer. Let the unpredictability become your ally, not your adversary, and watch your resilience propel you to new heights.

Learning from Setbacks

Setbacks in pickleball doubles aren't roadblocks but stepping stones to improvement. Take a look at how adopting a mindset that views setbacks as valuable lessons transforms every missed shot into an opportunity for growth.

- **Setbacks as Lessons:** A resilient mindset views setbacks not as failures but as valuable lessons. Every missed shot, every point lost, is an opportunity to learn, grow, and come back stronger.

- **Growth Mindset**: Cultivating a growth mindset is integral to using setbacks as stepping stones toward progress. Embracing challenges and viewing them as opportunities for development is a hallmark of mentally resilient players.

Learning from setbacks is an ongoing journey in the world of pickleball doubles. As you navigate the challenges, remember that setbacks are not roadblocks but guiding lights toward improvement. With a growth mindset, every setback becomes a setup for a comeback.

Trusting Your Partner and Communication

Pickleball doubles is a dance of coordination and trust between partners. Here's how building trust with your teammate and effective communication becomes the cornerstone of a resilient doubles team.

- **Building Connection**: Developing a strong connection with your teammate goes beyond understanding their playing style. It involves trust, effective communication, and a shared commitment to success.

- **Conflict Resolution:** Resilient teams don't shy away from conflicts. Instead, they turn disagreements into constructive discussions. Addressing issues promptly and finding solutions together strengthens the team's overall resilience.

Trust and communication form the heartbeat of successful pickleball doubles play. As you forge a strong connection with your partner, remember that effective communication and conflict resolution are the secret ingredients to a resilient and unbeatable team.

Visualization Techniques

The power of visualization extends beyond imagination. It's time to understand how visualization techniques help you see success and manifest it on the pickleball court.

- **Power of Visualization**: Visualization is a powerful mental tool. Resilient players leverage this technique to imagine flawless shots, seamless communication, and overall success on the court.

- **Pre-Match Visualization**: Before a match, visualize success. Picture yourself executing perfect shots, moving effortlessly across the court, and maintaining strong communication with your partner.
- **In-Match Visualization:** In the heat of the game, take a mental pause. Visualize overcoming obstacles, adapting to your opponent's strategies, and ultimately achieving success.

Visualization is your secret weapon in the arsenal of mental resilience. As you hone your ability to see success in your mind's eye, remember that what you visualize, you can actualize on the pickleball court.

Breathing Techniques for Calmness

In the whirlwind of pickleball doubles, maintaining composure is a superpower. Here are some simple yet effective breathing techniques to be your anchor, keeping you calm and collected under pressure:

- **Deep Breathing:** Incorporate deep, slow breaths into your routine to help regulate your nervous system. In moments of tension, taking a few deliberate breaths will reset your mental state.
- **Resetting Your Mind:** Inhale deeply, exhale slowly and reset your mental state. This simple yet effective technique will help you maintain focus and composure throughout the match.

Amidst the fast-paced rallies and high-stakes points, your breath is your constant companion. As you delve into the world of deep breathing, remember that calmness is not a luxury but a strategic advantage in the game of pickleball doubles.

Delving into these strategies and incorporating them into your game, you'll enhance your performance on the court and enjoy the game more fully. So, the next time you step onto the pickleball court, remember that building mental resilience is as essential as perfecting your shots.

Executing Strategies and Sharp Decision-Making

Pickleball is a strategic dance on the court where every move counts. Whether you're a novice or an experienced player, mastering the art of executing strategies and making quick decisions will take your game to the next level. In this section, you'll explore the thrilling world of pickleball strategies and decision-making, filled with insights and tips to elevate your gameplay.

The Dance of Strategies

Strategies in pickleball involve precise movements, thoughtful shot selections, and strategic court positioning. As you step onto the court, you journey through the fundamental techniques that form the bedrock of successful gameplay. It's time to explore the nuanced steps of this dance, from footwork essentials to the finesse of the third shot drop, as you choreograph your way to victory.

1. **Mastery of Fundamentals**: Achieving mastery in pickleball begins with a solid understanding of the fundamentals. A player's ability to execute precise shots, maintain effective court positioning,

and move seamlessly with agility lays the groundwork for strategic gameplay. The importance of footwork cannot be overstated, as it forms the basis for executing powerful shots and responding swiftly to opponents' moves.

2. **Serve Techniques:** The serve is the initiation of every rally in pickleball. As you advance, explore various serve techniques to add unpredictability to your game. From spin serves to power serves, each variation serves a specific purpose, keeping opponents guessing and giving you a crucial advantage.

3. **The Third Shot Drop**: The third shot drop is a strategic move that disrupts the opponent's momentum, setting the tone for controlled play. Exploring the nuances of the third shot will guide you in executing precise drops that force opponents into defensive positions, creating opportunities for offensive plays.

4. **Footwork and Positioning**: Nimble footwork and strategic positioning are the pillars of successful pickleball strategies. Learn to anticipate shots, cover the court effectively, and maintain optimal positioning to control the flow of the game. Understanding when to approach the net and when to defend from the baseline becomes an art in itself.

5. **Tactical Progression:** As you progress, incorporate advanced strategies into your gameplay. It includes deeper serves, strategic shot placement, and a keen understanding of your opponent's weaknesses. The emphasis shifts from

power to precision, with you making calculated moves to outsmart your adversaries.

As the final pops of the pickleball echo on the court, you'll find yourself executing movements and expressing strategic artistry. Mastery of fundamentals, finesse in serving, and strategic positioning become the strokes of the brush on this unique canvas. The ever-evolving and dynamic dance will leave you with a profound appreciation for the strategic tapestry woven into each match.

Decision-Making on the Fly

In the fast-paced games of pickleball, quick decision-making is a skill that distinguishes the exceptional from the proficient. Reading opponents, adapting mid-game, and effective communication between partners are the beats of this improvisational jazz. It's time to explore the dynamic world of decisions made in the heat of the rally, where split-second choices shape the game's narrative.

- **Reading Your Opponents:** The ability to read opponents is a hallmark of a skilled pickleball player. Understanding opponents' playing styles, strengths, and weaknesses allows you to tailor your strategies dynamically. Through keen observation, you adapt your gameplay to exploit vulnerabilities and gain a competitive edge.

- **Adapting Mid-Game:** Flexibility is a key attribute in the ever-changing landscape of a pickleball match. You must be adept at adapting your strategies mid-game based on evolving circumstances. Whether adjusting to an opponent's change in tactics or responding to unexpected challenges, quick thinking and adaptability become invaluable assets.

- **Effective Communication**: In doubles play, effective communication between partners is essential. Develop a system of clear signals and cues to coordinate your movements seamlessly. Communication becomes a strategic tool, allowing partners to synchronize their efforts and make split-second decisions that turn the game's tide.

- **Mind Games and Deception:** Strategic deception becomes a potent weapon in the player's arsenal. Through mind games and deceptive shots, you create uncertainty in your opponents' minds. Unexpected drops, spins, and angles add an element of unpredictability, making it challenging for opponents to anticipate and counteract strategic moves.

As the final point is scored, the symphony of decisions reaches its crescendo. Read your opponents like a well-worn novel, adapt strategies with the fluidity of a dancer, and communicate seamlessly with your partner. On the pickleball court, where every point is a plot twist, emerge as a tactician of the unexpected.

Mental Agility and Decision-Making

Beyond the physical demands, pickleball is a mental battleground where mental agility and decision-making reign supreme. Focused concentration, visualization techniques, and maintaining composure under pressure are the secret sauce behind every successful play. Here are some cognitive strategies to stay one step ahead in pickleball:

- **Focus and Concentration**: Maintaining unwavering focus is paramount in pickleball. Practice concentration techniques to eliminate distractions and stay present at each point. The ability to concentrate enhances decision-making, ensuring that you react swiftly and accurately to every situation on the court.

- **Visualization Techniques:** Visualization becomes a powerful tool for mental preparation. Adopt visualization techniques to mentally rehearse your strategies and decision-making processes. Envisioning successful plays and anticipating various scenarios enhances your on-court performance and bolsters your confidence.

- **Calm Under Pressure:** Pickleball often involves high-pressure situations, demanding players to remain calm and composed. Deep breathing exercises, mindfulness practices, and mental resilience training contribute to maintaining a calm demeanor under pressure. A composed mindset enhances decision-making clarity during critical moments in the match.

- **Learning from Mistakes:** Embracing mistakes as learning opportunities is fundamental to your development. Analyze errors, understand their root causes, and implement corrective measures for continuous improvement. Approach each mistake with a growth mindset, transforming setbacks into stepping stones toward excellence.

Mental agility and decision-making on the pickleball court transform your chances of success. Learning from mistakes is not just a tactic but a philosophy. You're now equipped with a strategic toolbox for future battles. As the final whistle blows, you'll find yourself stepping off the court physically exhausted yet mentally fortified.

Celebrating Success and Enjoying the Game

Amidst the strategic intensity, it's crucial not to lose sight of the joy that pickleball inherently brings. Celebrating success, acknowledging achievements, and relishing the journey contribute to a positive playing experience.

- **Acknowledging Achievements:** Celebrating successes, regardless of how small, contributes to a positive playing experience. Recognizing and acknowledging achievements, whether it be a well-executed shot or a strategic play, builds confidence and reinforces effective decision-making.

- **Enjoying the Journey:** Pickleball is a journey of continuous improvement and enjoyment. Relish every point, learn from every decision, and find joy in the camaraderie of the sport. The journey is as significant as the destination, and the love for the game will fuel your commitment to growth and excellence.

- **Positive Reinforcement:** Positive reinforcement of achievements, whether a well-executed shot or effective communication with your partner, reinforces a positive mindset. This reinforcement becomes a cornerstone of mental resilience.

- **Building Confidence**: Celebrating successes, big and small, contributes to building confidence. As you recognize your accomplishments, you reinforce the belief in your abilities, enhancing your mental resilience for future challenges.

As the echoes of the final match fade away, the essence of celebrating success and enjoying the game lingers. It's more than just tallying points. It's about recognizing growth, finding joy in the process, and relishing the camaraderie forged on the court. In the grand finale of celebrating success and enjoying the game, walk away as enthusiasts of the sport's infectious spirit.

The fusion of tactical mastery, adaptability, and mental resilience defines a successful pickleball player. Ultimately, the court is your canvas for strategic expression, and the joy of the game lies in the pursuit of excellence. Happy pickling!

Chapter 7: Advancing Your Skills in Double Play

To elevate your prowess in doubles play, incorporating strategic techniques and honing specific skills is paramount. Effective doubles strategies emphasize precise ball placement and control over raw power. Among other techniques, considering your partner's strengths and setting them up for success, commonly known as poaching, becomes a valuable skill to boost overall team performance.

This chapter is your passport to the next level of pickleball mastery. You'll navigate through strategic drills and engaging exercises for skill enhancement and explore how building consistency and confidence can elevate your doubles game. Incorporating these strategic insights and focusing on continuous practice and footwork improvement will help you advance your skills and thrive in the dynamic realm of pickleball doubles play.

Spice Up Your Pickleball Training: Dynamic Drills for Ultimate Fun

To truly shine on the court, you need to shake up your routine with dynamic drills that enhance your skills and add a dash of excitement to your game. Get ready to embark on a pickleball adventure with three high-energy drills. They're the turbo boost your game needs!

14. Drills can help you enhance your skills. Source: Thelyonhart, CC BY-SA 3.0 <https://creativecommons.org/licenses/by-sa/3.0>, via Wikimedia Commons: https://commons.wikimedia.org/wiki/File:Jeanpickle.jpg

Dynamic Dinking Drill

In the world of pickleball, finesse is the name of the game, and the Dynamic Dinking Drill is your backstage pass to mastering the dink dance. It's not just about gently tapping the ball over the net. It's about flaunting your control and finesse and making your opponent's waltz to your rhythm. Step up to the net and get this dink party started.

Step-by-Step Instructions:

1. **Positioning**: Strut your stuff at the kitchen line, ready to dazzle.
2. **Smooth Strikes:** Engage in a dink duel with your partner, grooving to the rhythm.
3. **Heightened Dinks:** Mix things up by changing the height of your dinks, **including low to high, and everything in between.**
4. **Lateral Shuffle:** Slide and glide along the kitchen line, hitting those dinks with flair.

Benefits:

- **Control Mastery**: Nail those dinks with finesse, becoming the control maestro of the court.
- **Reflex Razzle-Dazzle**: Boost your reflexes, responding to shots with a lightning-quick boogie.
- **Positioning Prowess**: Glide across the court with finesse, positioning yourself like a pickleball superstar.

The Dynamic Dinking Drill may seem like a smooth groove, but it's your ticket to pickleball stardom. Add this drill to your playlist, and watch as your opponent's trying to keep up with your dink disco.

Cross-Court Smash Challenge

If you think smashes are just for tennis, think again. The Cross-Court Smash Challenge is your invitation to the smash fiesta. It'll help you hit the ball hard and send it on a cross-court adventure that leaves your opponents bewildered. Get ready to unleash the smash beast.

Step-by-Step Instructions:

1. **Baseline Boogie**: Plant your feet at the baseline, ready for a smash showdown.
2. **Smash:** Launch powerful smashes, aiming for the farthest corners of the court.
3. **Switch It Up:** Show off your smash skills on both forehand and backhand sides.
4. **Intensity:** Gradually turn up the heat, unleashing smashes with escalating power.

Benefits:

- **Offensive Swagger:** Become the smash sensation, turning your opponents into spectators.
- **Versatility**: Smash from any court position, keeping your rivals guessing.
- **Strategic Smashes:** Keep your opponents on their toes with unexpected and powerful smashes.

The Cross-Court Smash Challenge injects a carnival atmosphere into your training routine while turning your smashes into a force to be reckoned with. Regular practice will refine your technique and make your smashes the life of the pickleball party.

Lob and Drop Shot Fusion

Ready to be the Picasso of pickleball? The Lob and Drop Shot Fusion is your artistic expression on the court. This tactical fusion combines the elegance of lobs with the finesse of drop shots, creating a masterpiece that will leave your opponents in awe.

Step-by-Step Instructions:

1. **Lob:** Start with baseline lobs, sending the ball soaring high over the net.
2. **Net Waltz:** Swiftly move to the non-volley zone after your elegant lob performance.
3. **Drop Shot:** Follow up with a drop shot, delicately placing the ball in the kitchen.
4. **Rhythm Fusion:** Dance between baseline lobs and net drop shots, creating a mesmerizing fusion.

Benefits:

- **Strategic Transitions:** Master the art of transitioning between offensive lobs and delicate drop shots.
- **Court Awareness**: Sharpen your awareness of court positioning and timing, essential for executing this fusion with finesse.
- **Tactical Tapestry:** Confuse and outmaneuver opponents with an unpredictable fusion of shot selections.

The Lob and Drop Shot Fusion is your masterpiece in the making. Embracing this fusion regularly will refine your ability to transition between contrasting shots and develop a deeper understanding of court dynamics.

Incorporate these dance-worthy drills into your pickleball practice, and you'll find yourself grooving to success on the court. Whether you're a dink maestro, a smash sensation, or a court artist, these dynamic drills will elevate your game, making you the star of the pickleball dance floor.

Building Consistency and Confidence

Pickleball is a rapidly growing sport that has captured the hearts of players, young and old. As you step onto the court, the key to success lies in two pillars: consistency and confidence. Here's how mastering these elements significantly enhances your pickleball experience.

Understanding Pickleball Basics

Before you dive into the nuances of consistency and confidence, it's best to lay a solid foundation by revising the basics of pickleball. From court dimensions to the paddle grip, this section will summarize the fundamentals, setting the stage for your journey to pickleball mastery.

- **Know Your Court:** To navigate the pickleball court effectively, understanding its dimensions is crucial. The 20x44-foot court is divided into service and non-volley zones. Mastering court boundaries allows strategic plays and ensures you're always one step ahead.

- **Mastering the Paddle Grip:** The foundation of control in pickleball lies in the paddle grip.

Experiment with various grips to find what suits you best. Whether it's the Eastern, Western, or Continental grip, each affects your shots differently. Precision starts with the right grip.

- **Scoring Simplified:** Pickleball's scoring system might seem intricate initially, but it's straightforward. Points are scored only by the serving team, and games usually go up to 11 points. Stay vigilant and keep track of the score with each rally.

Building Consistency

Consistency is the heartbeat of a successful pickleball player. From perfecting the serve to mastering the dink shot, each aspect plays a pivotal role in ensuring you maintain control and precision on the court.

- **Perfecting the Serve:** The serve sets the tone for the game. Aim for a consistent and controlled serve. Practice different types of serves, from the basic drive to the tricky spin serve. Surprise your opponents and keep them guessing.

- **Mastering the Dink Shot:** The dink shot is a finesse move crucial for maintaining consistency. Practice controlled, soft shots close to the net. Developing this skill ensures you confidently handle fast-paced exchanges and control the game's pace.

- **Footwork Fundamentals:** Your footwork is the backbone of consistency. Position yourself strategically to respond effectively to opponents' shots. Engage in drills to improve agility, allowing you to reach the ball with ease and maintain control.

Boosting Confidence

Confidence transforms good players into great ones. Here, you'll unravel the psychology behind confidence in pickleball. Visualization techniques, positive self-talk, and learning from mistakes are the building blocks to fortifying your confidence and enhancing your overall performance.

15. *Confidence can turn good players into great ones. Source: https://www.pexels.com/photo/photo-of-woman-in-yellow-turtleneck-sweater-blue-denim-jeans-and-glasses-giving-the-thumbs-up-3768997/*

- **Visualization Techniques**: Picture success before it happens. Visualization is a powerful tool to boost confidence. Envision successful serves and precise shots. Incorporate visualization into your pre-game routine for a mental edge.

- **Positive Self-Talk:** Your mind can be your greatest ally. Develop a habit of positive self-talk on the court. Create a repertoire of affirmations such as "I can do this" or "Every point is an opportunity." Confidence follows positive thoughts.

- **Learn from Mistakes:** Mistakes are part of the game. Embrace them as learning opportunities. Analyze what went wrong and adjust your strategy. Every setback is a chance to grow and become a more confident player.

Mental Toughness on the Court

Pickleball is not just a physical game. It's also a mental challenge. Mental fortitude is required to stay focused, handle pressure, and navigate the complexities of the game with ease. Strengthen your mind, and you'll find your on-court prowess reaching new heights.

- **Focus and Concentration**: Maintaining focus during intense rallies is a game-changer. Train your mind to stay in the present moment. Mindfulness exercises will enhance your concentration, ensuring you don't miss a beat.

- **Handling Pressure Situations:** Pickleball often involves high-pressure moments. Develop strategies to manage stress during crucial points. Deep breathing exercises will help you stay calm and composed, enhancing your decision-making under pressure.

Game Strategy for Consistency and Confidence

Understanding your opponents and fostering effective team communication are the cornerstones of strategic gameplay. Here are some game strategies to complement your quest for consistency and confidence, turning each match into a strategic combo of skill and intuition.

- **Knowing Your Opponent:** Understanding your opponent's playing style is a strategic advantage. Adapt your gameplay to exploit their weaknesses. Whether they prefer aggressive smashes or finesse shots, knowing their tendencies will give you the upper hand.

- **Team Communication**: In doubles, effective communication with your partner is paramount. Develop a synchronized game plan, communicate your intentions, and support each other on the court. A cohesive team enhances consistency and confidence.

As you conclude this journey into mastering pickleball, remember that consistency and confidence are not acquired overnight. Practice these strategies diligently, and with time, you'll find yourself dominating the court with finesse and flair. Embrace the joy of the game, and let each point be a stepping stone towards pickleball greatness.

Chapter 8: Beyond the Basics: Playing Smart and Winning

In the dynamic realm of pickleball, transcending the basics is a requisite for those seeking not just to play but to dominate. This final chapter delves into the nuanced strategies that will propel your game to new heights. This chapter is your golden ticket to playing like a pro and leaving your opponents scratching their heads. You're diving into the exciting world of advanced strategies for competitive doubles to outsmart opponents. Get your game face on because it's about to get spicy.

Advanced Strategies for Competitive Doubles

Pickleball, the quirky lovechild of tennis and ping pong, requires proper strategies to outmaneuver opponents. You're about to discover some top-secret strategies to leave your opponents scratching their heads. From the Fake Fumble to the Switcheroo Smash and the Mirror Effect, you'll explore a playbook to turn your doubles game into a dazzling display of finesse and trickery. Get ready to bring some spice to the court and keep your rivals guessing.

16. Learning advanced strategies can help you play pickleball competitively. Source: Bryceppa, CC BY-SA 4.0 <https://creativecommons.org/licenses/by-sa/4.0>, via Wikimedia Commons: https://commons.wikimedia.org/wiki/File:Simone_Jardim_and_Lucy_Kovalova.jpg

The Fake Fumble

Who said fumbles are a bad thing? In pickleball, a well-timed Fake Fumble is the secret weapon to make your opponents second-guess everything. It's a magic trick but with a paddle.

Step-by-Step Instructions:

1. **Act Like a Magician:** Start a rally and subtly pretend you've lost control of the ball.

2. **Abracadabra:** Watch your opponent fall for the act and relax their guard.

3. **Watch Them Fall**: Seize the moment of confusion to deliver a shot that'll leave them mystified.

The key to a successful Fake Fumble is in the theatrics. Master the art of subtle deception, make your opponents believe they've cracked your code, and then unveil a shot that defies their expectations. This strategy is a psychological masterpiece that turns your opponents into unwitting participants in your pickleball magic show.

The Switcheroo Smash

Why settle for predictability when you can dazzle with the Switcheroo Smash? It's the pickleball version of a plot twist that keeps opponents on their toes.

Step-by-Step Instructions:

1. **Smash the Norm:** Hit them with a power smash that says, "I mean business!"

2. **Twist and Shout:** Instead of another power move, switch to finesse like a ninja in disguise.

3. **Keep Them Guessing**: Dance between power and finesse to keep opponents scratching their heads.

The art of the Switcheroo Smash lies in the unexpected transition from power to finesse. Create an illusion of predictability and then shatter it. The sudden switch confuses opponents, making them question their defensive strategies.

The Mirror Effect

Mimic your opponent's playing style and shots, confusing them with their tactics. The Mirror Effect turns you and your partner into a synchronized duo, gliding across the court in perfect harmony. It's not a dance, but it sure feels like one.

Step-by-Step Instructions:

1. **Sync or Swim:** Communicate with your partner to initiate the Mirror Effect.

2. **Mirror, Mirror on the Court**: Observe your opponents' patterns and replicate their moves, then switch them up for unpredictability. Move in sync with your partner, covering the court like a dynamic duo.

3. **Anticipate Together:** With synchronized movements, read opponents' shots like you're psychic.

The beauty of the Mirror Effect lies in the seamless communication between partners. Mimic each other's movements and anticipate the next step without uttering a word. This strategy transforms the doubles game into a choreographed dance, where partners move as one entity.

Now, you're armed with the clandestine moves to transform your pickleball doubles game into a spectacle of deception and brilliance. These strategies are your secret tickets to pickleball stardom. Step onto the court, be the puppet master of the pickleball matrix, and watch as opponents marvel at your unpredictable finesse.

Strategies to Outsmart Opponents and Secure Victory

Pickleball, the sport that combines finesse, strategy, and a touch of humor, is a game of wits as much as it is about skill. As you step onto the court, armed with a paddle and a determination to outsmart your opponents, consider adding a touch of mystery to your game. Here are some clandestine strategies to make you the puppet master of the pickleball court. These strategies go beyond the typical playbook, introducing an element of surprise to keep your opponents on their toes.

The Invisible Net Master

Your opponent is standing at the net, ready to block your every move. Now imagine making the net disappear right before their eyes. That's the magic of The Invisible Net Master.

Step-by-Step Instructions:
1. **The Paddle Wand:** Hold your paddle with a relaxed grip, concealing your intentions.
2. **The Deceptive Dink:** Execute a dink shot as if aiming for the net.

3. **Switch:** At the last moment, redirect the ball away from the net, leaving opponents baffled. Surprise opponents with low shots or unexpected lobs, exploiting their anticipation.

Benefits:

- **Confusion Is Key:** Keep opponents guessing with a disappearing act they won't see coming.
- **Opening for Attack:** Use their hesitation to launch an unexpected offensive.

The Invisible Net Master defies the laws of physics and creates doubt in the minds of your opponents. As they question the very existence of the net, you'll be setting the stage for a victorious performance.

The Whispering Wind

In pickleball, strategy and finesse intertwine, and the Whispering Wind emerges as a silent orchestra of communication. This strategy invites players to transcend verbal exchanges and utilize non-verbal cues, creating an intricate dance of hand signals and gestures.

Step-by-Step Instructions:

1. **Non-Verbal Communication:** Establish a secret language with your partner, using subtle hand signals and gestures.
2. **Darkened Game Plan:** Keep opponents in the dark by avoiding verbal communication about your on-court tactics.

3. **Element of Surprise**: Execute plays without verbal cues, enhancing the surprise factor and leaving opponents guessing.

Benefits:

- **Enhanced Teamwork:** The Whispering Wind cultivates a deeper connection between partners, fostering seamless coordination.
- **Decoding Prevention:** Communicating silently prevents opponents from deciphering your game plan, allowing you a strategic advantage.
- **Mysterious Aura:** Infuse the court with an air of mystery as your silent communication becomes a captivating element of the game.

The Whispering Wind strategy makes silent communication a powerful tool. The strategy elevates teamwork and ensures that opponents remain in the dark, unable to decode the intricate maneuvers unfolding before them. With this technique, the match transforms into a dance of mystery and coordination, where every silent gesture speaks volumes.

The Phantom Serve

What if your serve could be a phantom, appearing out of nowhere? The Phantom Serve is the ace up your sleeve that keeps opponents searching for a ball that seemingly materializes from thin air.

Step-by-Step Instructions:

1. **Stealthy Stance:** Assume a nonchalant serving position, giving no hint of your intentions.

2. **The Sleight of Hand**: Use a quick and unexpected motion to disguise the serve.

3. **Serve and Disappear**: Execute a serve that seems to materialize mysteriously, leaving opponents flat-footed.

Benefits:

- **Serve Unseen**: Catch opponents off-guard with a serve they can't anticipate.
- **Control the Tempo**: Set the pace of the game by maintaining the element of surprise.

With the Phantom Serve, you're serving a riddle. Watch as opponents struggle to decode the mystery of your serves, giving you a strategic edge on the court.

In the playful world of pickleball, mastering these covert strategies transforms you into a sorcerer of the court. These tactics are an invitation to dance with unpredictability and emerge victorious. As you weave these mystical moves into your game, relish the joy of surprising opponents, leaving them spellbound by your mastery. So, grab your paddle, step onto the court, and let the pickleball sorcery begin.

Conclusion

As you bid adieu to the thrilling pages of "Pickleball Strategy and Doubles," roll up your sleeves and dive into the juiciest takeaways that have transformed you into the ultimate pickleball maestro. Ready for the ride? Here's your backstage pass to the blockbuster of doubles play:

Key Takeaways

- **The Basics of Pickleball**: Lay a strong foundation by understanding the rules, court dynamics, and essential equipment, ensuring a solid starting point for players at any level.

- **Equipping for Double Play**: Delve into the nuances of choosing the right partner, understanding their strengths, and fostering effective communication, crucial elements in the success of doubles play.

- **The Fundamentals of Double Play:** Master footwork, positioning, and shot selection, honing the core skills that elevate doubles performance to peak levels.

- **Pickleball Strategies and Tactics**: Outsmart opponents, unleash surprise attacks, and leave them scratching their heads with your genius plays.
- **Developing Racket Techniques:** Fine-tune racket skills, including grip, swing, and control, enhancing precision and power in every shot.
- **The Mental Game and Strategy Execution**: Time to channel your inner Zen master. Master focus and resilience, and execute strategies with finesse for a well-rounded and competitive gameplay.
- **Advancing Your Skills in Double Play:** Elevate your game by refining techniques, incorporating advanced strategies, and adapting to various playing styles, ensuring continuous improvement.
- **Beyond the Basics: Playing Smart and Winning**: Level up, Sherlock! It's time to deduce opponents' moves, make smart choices, and bask in the glory of victory like the pickleball detective you are.

Hold your pickleball paddles, folks! Before you go conquer the pickleball universe, how about sharing the love? If this book has been your pickleball sidekick, sprinkle a bit of that good vibe in the reviews. Your words will spark joy in the hearts of fellow players and keep the pickleball party rolling. Until your next pickleball rendezvous, keep swinging, smashing, and dinking like there's no tomorrow. Cheers to the sweet taste of victory and the never-ending fun of pickleball!

References

JustPaddles. (2023, September 15). Pickleball doubles. JustPaddles.
https://www.justpaddles.com/blog/post/pickleball-doubles/

Kenniston, B. (2023, May 4). Pickleball doubles rules – how to play the game. Pickleheads.
https://www.pickleheads.com/guides/pickleball-doubles-rules

Patton, E. (2020, October 25). Rules of pickleball and singles & doubles scoring. Onix Pickleball.
https://www.onixpickleball.com/blogs/learn-pickleball/how-to-keep-score-in-sport-of-pickleball

Pickleball. (n.d.). Msu.edu.
https://recsports.msu.edu/imsports/activityrules/pickleball.html

Pickleball Doubles Rule Basics. (n.d.). Iastate.edu.
https://im.recservices.iastate.edu/download-file.php?id=2719

Pickleball doubles rules. (n.d.-a). Pickleball-paddles.com.
https://www.pickleball-paddles.com/pages/pickleball-doubles-rules

Pickleball doubles rules. (n.d.-b). Recreational Services | Cornell University. https://scl.cornell.edu/recreation/sports-equipment/intramural-sports/policies-rules/pickleball-doubles-rules

Pickleball rules. (2023, September 1). Lawn Tennis Association. https://www.lta.org.uk/play/ways-to-play/pickleball/pickleball-rules/

Rules summary. (n.d.). Usapickleball.org. https://usapickleball.org/what-is-pickleball/official-rules/rules-summary

Printed in Dunstable, United Kingdom